D1570106

Treasure Hunting on a Budget

Finding a Fortune without Spending a Fortune

By Robert E. Park

Treasure Hunting on a Budget

Finding a Fortune without Spending a Fortune

ISBN 0-7414-1905-X

Published by:

PUBLISHING.COM

519 West Lancaster Avenue
Haverford, PA 19041-1413
Info@buybooksontheweb.com
www.buybooksontheweb.com
Toll-free (877) BUY BOOK
Local Phone (610) 520-2500
Fax (610) 519-0261

Printed in the United States of America

Printed on Recycled Paper

Published January 2004

ACKNOWLEDGMENTS

I would like to thank all the people who worked with me along the way, including everyone from the fellow who sold me the first detector, to my family, who tolerated my obsession with treasure hunting.

Special thanks to my lovely wife Patty, for her patience, understanding, and for helping even when she didn't understand. I thank my sons Justin and Patrick for their immeasurable help and assistance in the making of this book and for helping to get my equipment to the search site.

To my friends and those who think metal detecting is an important part of their lives.

To the dreamer in us all.

CONTENTS

Introduction

This book, on Treasure Hunting, is about doing just that, on or within a budget. It is about finding treasure seen and unseen, valuables hidden or lost, goodies easily accessible and those harder to get to. It is about doing a complete examination of a property with an electronic metal detector and using your eyes and imagination. It is about making money from a hobby and doing so in areas that other people overlook.

Few adventures stimulate men's minds more than the search for treasure. From the earliest inkling of mans history, men have sought that which was lost or collected by others before them. Ancient man craved finding what great treasures were collected before him, on down the line. The Greeks, Romans, Europeans, and Spanish, all in their turn, conquered and took the riches they desired. Vast wealth has been buried and hidden to prevent it from falling into the hands of the conquerors. This has gone on for thousands of years, in the civilized world and uncivilized alike. North America has had its fair share of discovery and conflict as well, thousands of years of it. We only recognize the past seven hundred years or so, but, there are those who believe the Americas were visited by Phoenician and Carthaginian sailors three thousand years before Columbus. Historic evidence supports this, as much as it does the known Spanish Conquest of South America and Mexico and south and southwest United States.

Where there is conflict, there is loss; loss of life, culture, art and the loss of wealth. No place is this more true than Mexico and the Americas. Greed motivated one culture to conquer another throughout history. Much of this was carried out by Jesuit and Franciscan Priests against the Indians of the Southwest. Old furnaces and slag dumps near mission ruins and caved-in shafts or tunnels are mute testimony to their cruel use of the indigenous population. These operations were carried out for many years, a fact well authenticated in the Archives of Spain and Mexico.

Still others prayed on coastal trade such as Pirates and buccaneers, who for centuries ventured to where the winds would take them. America is blessed with many miles of coast which offered refuge to these rebels of no Nation. As many legions of treasure exist so does coastal mile. During the Golden age of Piracy, little separated the legal taking of cargo by Privateers, or the looting by Pirates, and one often lead to the other. Regardless of deception, most favored the shallow inlets along the Carolina coast, Virginia, Georgia and Florida. Vast wealth still lay's buried in the sands and shallow waters there.

The Civil War was the United States last conflict on its' own soil, and accounts for Billions in value of gold and silver coinage and house wares lost. Most of this was lost forever when those who buried it were killed, whether killed in the conflict itself or the looting afterwards. Most of these types of caches are found today by accident than by any other way. Building and renovation in the Eastern Seaboard area can uncover unsuspected wealth as often as not.

All early American waterways were the super highway of its' day. Commerce, trade and travel depended on them heavily. Wharfs and towns sprang-up at major crossings and experienced a rebirth with the coming of the Railroad. Every change created a chance for something of value to be lost. The great wanderers in American history transported something of value back and forth across this country constantly. Even the Great Depression created lost wealth somewhere. People have always lost things and always will.

If people lose things or hide them by nature, then others can find them by using knowledge, determination, and exploitation of technology. This type of individual is naturally drawn to seek that which is lost, and only lacks the knowledge of where to begin to search.

There is something exciting and romantic about seeking the noble metals. The search and hardships are somehow less hardened when the discovery is made. The breeze is cooler and the air smells fresher. Old men feel younger and young men feel vibrant. It's the small conquest with its tangible results which is the real reward. You may not find a treasure chest full of gold and silver coins, chains and rings but, over the life of this hobby and adventure, you can fill your own chest of treasures. Find just 5 or 6 pieces of silver and 1 or 2 pieces of gold per month and you can amass quite a collection. The rewards are still out there and just waiting to be found.

The majority of treasure hunters are independent, self-reliant and adventuresome souls, with much of the vigor and courage of our pioneering forefathers. They are individuals who have remained true to the basic concepts of human worth and self-respect. But...you probably know that.

Chapter One: Dump Digging

Treasure hunting... just the mention of these words quickens the pulse and kicks the imagination into high gear. The treasure hunter is often seen as an obsessive dreamer, a reckless adventurer who has little or no investment in the treasure he finds. But, the successful treasure hunter researches his area of interest. The most important thing is that he invests only what he can afford and not become compulsive in his pursuit of treasure.

The unbelievable amount of equipment available to the treasure hunters is mind boggling. Metal detectors, recovery tools, deep scanners, infrared scanners and magnetometers are just some of the tools available. The list goes on and can often set the committed treasure hunter back more than he can afford. There is no need to spend a fortune in our endeavor for treasure. We can start with what we can afford and slowly improve our equipment as our skills, talent and luck improve. And, as we find items of value, we can then turn that back into working capital.

Because dump digging is the easiest to do, with little equipment, and can be done alone or with the whole family, it is a logical start for the beginner. As a child I remember Bottle digging with my family on many trips. Mom was the spark-plug of this adventure, but we all (four boys and Dad) took to it as ducks to water. We'd walk miles of Railroad tracks for insulators, dig in long forgotten dumps for bottles, and hunt sand dunes for bottle works plants. With garden hoes and hand trowels, we would move large amounts of earth to unveil glass treasures long forgotten. Sometimes construction would uncover forgotten dumps and allow us to "weekend" hunt to our hearts contents. I remember many wonderful hours seeking "who knows what would pop-up next", much of which still is displayed at my folks home.

Just another day at the beach....sun, sand, and good exercise- with a few finds.

Since those days I've fallen back on dump digging as a "back-up" to treasure hunting. With new ideas and equipment, I've gleaned even more from this activity. Employing screens (different sizes and shapes for different reasons) I now find, along with bottles: coins, tokens, luggage tags, dog tags (1890's), buttons, marbles, and many old doll parts. Best of all, this hobby is best done in the late fall or winter, when snakes and insects are dormant. Don't forget to wear coveralls to stay clean and keep warm. While other treasure hunting activities stop in winter, dump digging is at its best. Of course, you could do research on those cold, overcast days, but some will search. And once you've found some "jewels", bitters bottles, cures, or ink wells- you'll search for more. I once found a silver belt buckle weighing 2 ½ oz. But a simple porcelain doll hand or leg may be worth far more.

My favorite tools include garden trowels, a short handled hoe (because you will be on your knees or in a hole), an Army "E" tool, a large screw driver, and ½ inch hail screen or hardware cloth on some sort of frame. For your exploratory work, a narrow screen may work best. My best screen is flat in front, growing deeper in the back, forming a 2 or 3 inch catch at the back. It is only 10 inches wide by almost 24 inches long and looks like a paint roller pan made entirely from a ½ inch screen. Most items of value will stay in this size screen, but you may want to place some ¼ inch screen in one corner or at the front to catch smaller size items. I do this with my water detecting screen and it catches small earrings and charms along with 22 cal. bullets, and cases, and tiny sterling loops etc.

So, how do we start? You should already have a place in mind. But if you don't, try to find a spot with rotten cans and broken glass. It would be good to research some historic or interesting sites within your area. Once you find your place, develop a hole or ditch and work it into and through your screen. Shake out the dirt, and carefully search what remains. Then discard and repeat.

This works best in areas that are very junky of course, because people brought the junk there in the first place. Put your goodies in a nail apron or "war" bag and move the junk so that it will not get discovered again. This is a dump, so I'm not saying you must remove all junk that you will find, like you would be doing if you were detecting or prospecting because the rotten cans alone would cripple you. But make sure you fill in all of your holes and cover this junk back up to keep from injuring someone.

If you're lucky, you'll uncover a large amount of colored glass. Try to locate the local artisan's and see if any of the stain-glass people are interested in the finer colored glass. You may able to sell it or trade it out. They like flat pieces with bright colors, especially glorious blue.

Different types of screens can be made cheaply and easily to suit any treasure hunting need. Large dished sifters can be used for dump digging or under dried-out swimming holes. Floating screens are mainly for water detecting, but can be set-up under your dredge discharge to catch items that flow off of the dredge. Flat picture-flame sifters work well for detecting in dry sandy areas and very shallow water. Sifters can help speed-up target recovery and are very useful in extremely trashy areas.

As mentioned before, doll parts will probably be found from time to time. I call them parts because old dolls had only porcelain heads, hands on short arms, and legs from the knees down to simple flat feet. The rest was made of cloth stuffed with more cloth. I found a bunch of this for a couple of years before I realized their value.

Old dolls sell for thousands of dollars and people will create or repair them if they have the parts. I traded a small box of these parts to a "Doll Lady" and she almost passed out. She couldn't imagine that they were found without expensive equipment or any real skill, over a short period of time. The internet would be the perfect market for these items.

4

The farther North and East that you are, the better your dumps will be. Many folks in the past would dump their garbage into depressions or gullies along rivers. These in turn, filled over with run-off or flooding and are now below grade. Use a metal rod with a "T" handle or bent in a "L" (on top) to probe for metal or glass. This will save you from digging in an unproductive area. People also used the river to dump into and sometimes the currents moved their garbage on down stream. This would hang-up in low areas, holes and drop-offs just like gold will in gold barring areas.

Most old towns and cities in the West were (or are) located on rivers and will have bottle dumps in areas outside of its old city limits. These areas now are inside those limits and easy to find with old maps. Look for undeveloped areas in the older Downtown areas first. Older city Parks have shrunk, sometimes due to the cost of keeping them up. Hunt the hill tops and slope fronts, and definitely the long over grown hedge or boundary vegetation.

Really old dump sites can hide many artifacts, relics, clay bricks, or even Indian artifacts. Many metal objects were made of copper, brass, bronze, silver and even gold.

Some were not intended to be thrown away, but were by accident. Many accidents claimed the lives of drifters or cowhands, and if sickness was involved, personal items would be disposed of.

Many, many homes and business were damaged or destroyed by war.

The War of Independence, the Spanish/ American War, the War of 1812, and the Civil War destroyed vast amounts of wealth. Often the rebuilders simply cleared away wreckage to start over. This still happens today after flooding and storm damage. Vast forest fires wipe out entire homesteads without a trace. Where does all of our stuff go? To quote a friend, "Under all is the land." pretty much covers that.

5

These same wars account for a great deal of purposely hidden wealth, most with the hope of being recovered, and many not. If the War didn't wipe-out the people, it did their property. Huge amounts of wealth were never recovered and exist to this day.

There are also dumps associated with old mining operations. These include waste rock and daily household items, both of which offer great opportunities. There is no telling what you can find here.

Most waste rock was eyeballed for value in a time before metal detectors and present technology, which you can use to your advantage. Research will uncover many abandoned mines, mining camps, and the towns that sprang up around them. All will have their dumps.

Once you have found a dump and worked it, you will know where to return to years later, with better equipment and skills developed first, from this simple and cheap method of treasure hunting.

HINT: Dropped items often collect around the older Downtown buildings that have air vent grids or grating along storefronts and entries. These fill with dirt and material and also dropped coins and other items. They are usually locked and haven't been cleaned in years because they are no longer in use to heat and cool the business. Offer to clean this area out. Clean out with a shovel into a 5 gallon bucket and screen later at home to recover what value may be there. You may want to do this on a regular basis for the business owners.

Dear IRS,
Please remove me from your mailing list.

Chapter Two: Coin Shooting

This method of Treasure-Hunting, also known as metal detecting, is my second love, and is still my main money return. My first detector, bought with hard earned money, was purchased while I was still in High School. It was the latest TR detector available and very disappointing. I pawned it to eat after I graduated and moved out on my own. Years later, I bought a White's 6000, discriminator model and fell in love. It and the next detector paid for themselves six times over. Buying a New metal detector may be one of life's greatest pleasures, because I always seem to have three or four of them.

While I may have 20 plus years of experience with detectors, I can not do the subject justice in one small chapter. Whole books by far better people are dedicated to this treasure hunting device. Authors like Charles Garett and others, have numerous books in great detail on the operation and methods of detecting. They cover finding locations to using your detector, improving your chances of success, tuning, and how their type of detector works. I have these in my home library for research and refreshing my memory. You can never have too many resource books. Each author has data that I hadn't thought of until I read their books. These books are a wealth of information and are a treasure in themselves. Check out EBay and see how cheap (and sometimes how expensive) these great books can be bought. I've been accumulating Treasure books of both Sea Coast to have for retirement and my great treasure hunt!

What I can contribute is that you can never dig too much trash. The good stuff is under the trash that others have past over. If you find an old, popular area full of trash, you've found a popular place that valuables have collected also.

Remember that valuable metals are heavy and sink into the earth, as well as get covered with everything else. I use to pass these up too, to hunt easier places. Almost by accident I found goodies while sifting up a bunch of pull tabs and other junk. The deeper I dug, the better the finds became. I found that I wasn't even using the detector. After I picked all visible trash and raking up more trash, I sifted up a bunch more trash. That's when I could finally use the detector. Of course, this is like dump digging, but that's where this skill developed, I'm sure.

This means digging trash whereever you detect, especially those older abandoned homestead, town sites, older parks and swimming areas, and stores and trade areas.

We have an old impoundment swimming area, a dammed river that has been popular since the 1930's through the late 70's. We also had a drought. Those two occurrences should make any Treasure Hunter motivated. I now had an exposed river bottom, where people had swam, fished, partied and all-around had a good time. The buried steel, aluminum can pull tabs, fishing weights and other junk were unbelievable. After filling a garbage bag with trash and removing it, I began detecting with some discrimination and removing junk and the occasional goody. By the end of a hot sweaty day, I had an apron full of trash and treasure, broken glass and gold. It took all summer, all fall and many trips thru the winter to hunt this site. I still hunt this site and should have new exposure this summer. Also, remember this, I wasn't the first to detect this place. There were dig holes and discarded trash by those same holes. I found a 1959 men's class ring beside and under one of those dig holes- after removing the trash.

The junky areas had the best finds. The two diving platforms, (dilapidated), rope swing, and Dam wall had attracted the most people. People, after all, lose the stuff other people seek.

In the beginning, many years ago, still with some great finds. The key to the early success was investing a great amount of time to the hobby. The really great finds were also easier to make in the early years....but are still possible with research and time in the field.

Another observation is that coins and such items seem to beg to be dug up after a heavy rain or any soaking rains that last for days. After all, we are dealing with electrically transmitted waves into a medium (the ground), that resists, limiting depth. That is why the signal doesn't go very far, say, 5 to 8 inches if we are lucky. The max depth is at the very center of the search coil, going down in a cone-shape. So if you aren't overlapping your sweeps, then you aren't covering all of the area at that max depth either. With a wet or moist medium (the ground), the signal moves quicker and farther with less resistance.

Also, coins leach out metal residue creating a halo around them. Gold doesn't do this, but all others do. This halo becomes moist and helps to make the target appear larger and easier to locate.

You must over lap each pass of the search coil to utilize their maximum penetration. All books on detecting will tell you this. This is important, because unless you are using a "DD", double D coil, the concentric coil only sees the greatest depth at its center. With an 8 inch coil, you could miss a coin at 6 inch depth by 3 inches on both sides by not overlapping.

No matter what brand, type or cost of your detector, you must become the greatest operator of that machine. You must read your owners manual. Read it until you truly understand it and operate the machine as they are demonstrating in the manual. Learn how to tune your detector and use all of its features.

The newer and more expensive the unit is, the more features it will have. Manuals will offer tips that will help you get started and keep hunting. The hardest thing is always having a place to hunt. So, always have a list of possible hunt locations, keep adding to the list, always have a list.

The metal detector can do great things, but can't find anything in your closet. That is why the user needs to get off to a good start. If you are using an inexpensive machine often with a good understanding, then you are probably out performing the folks with expensive units that are not used as often. I've seen this many times. For example, a guy with a Radio Shack discontinued model skunks a guy using a $1200 Minelab, at the same place. You use your unit and wear-out a coil cover and 100's of batteries and you'll be the best in your field. You will probably be moving up to better models also.

Many metal detector users do not keep a record or logbook of their finds. The dealer who sold me my first detector recommended this 20 plus years ago and I followed his advice. I learned much from his experience and this was probably his best advice. How else would you know how well you were doing? Why could I not use this to keep track of productive areas and develop new areas to hunt?

Recently others have recommended keeping a log with more detail than just numbers, locations, and types of finds. Things such as weather conditions, equipment type, settings, and additional comments could also be included. Looking back I can see the importance in this type of information and would do that if I had it to do over. After 20,000 coins and 1600 jewelry items or relics, my simple Log is huge as it is. What is more important here is to keep a record of your success and development as a metal detectorist, or prospector or whatever it is that you excel at.

HOTSPOTS:

After years of hunting you know these areas right off the bat, when you see them (in a yard for example). They are the driveways and the sidewalks in front, if the house has one. This was my specialty for years, until I ran out of area (but always on the lookout for new areas).

Many times you can just get out very early and search a couple of blocks of sidewalks before too many curious people slow you to a stop. Seek out the oldest neighborhood first. This is also public easement, where the city signage is, city utilities, mail boxes and water meters are located, and no one has the right to ask you to stop. You will find people out there, who think they own this area and will ask you to leave. You handle this your own way, but beware of it.

11

Other hot spots are a beaten path around to the other side of the house (It's there, look for a slight depression going around the corners). Follow this around to the clothesline in the backyard, the path to the alley or garbage offset. Look for any yard toys or playground equipment. A grape arbor or big shade tree framed out with Lilacs or some other perennials is another place folks might gather in the cool of the evening to relax, in a time before air-conditioning.

Wells and outhouses are a must (if you are so lucky) inside and out. Many daily routines involved both of these fixtures. Also, check the path from these locations to the house.

Look in and around the vegetable patch, because Mother may have hidden her butter and egg money there.

 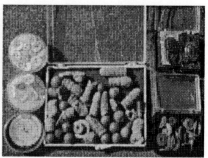

Examples of the some of the "treasure" found while detecting.

She would be there daily and expected to be digging and poking around. She could add or subtract from her bank here without raising suspicion. Here would also be easy digging with easy land marks. God knows Mother needed something to be easy.

Now, for other "land marks". People needed land marks, per say, in the yard, just as man has always needed something with which to mark his location. This would help him find his cache in the dark- because they mostly accessed their "banks" under cover of night or early morning.

Concentrate on large trees, grape arbors, clothe lines, pump houses, bird baths, statuses, flagstone paths (paving) and anything set-in the area to stay. Large trees have been known to have nails (or brass spikes) driven into them as markers. They could also suspend a string or line from that nail if it were on a limb and it would hang above their cache. There are whole books written on this subject, so check them out, I've listed some good pubs. in the back of this book. After a number of these types of searches you will know where to look first, and then detect the remainder of the area if you have more time. Keep this information in your Logbook as a possible search location for later use, under different conditions, like equipment or soil conditions.

This should give some idea as to the need of a "war bag". This is any small to medium backpack or tool bag or even a utility belt. Form follows function here, but you must keep it simple. Start with gloves and garbage bags for trash and treasure or rain gear. An extra set of batteries is a must, as well as a small folding shovel and drinking water, and maybe a handkerchief to wipe sweat from your face or to clean your glasses. This bag should be big enough to carry these items but small enough not to get in your way or wear you out carrying it. Once developed, it will contain your favorite digging tools and always be ready to take to the field when you grab your detector to go searching. This way, you will always have the items needed to be successful.

Keep this in mind...

What we find and what we search for can differ greatly. Sometimes we may find the unexpected, like dog tags, tokens, slave tags, luggage tags (once nailed to trunks for travel) or military items. All of these are great finds and you should keep and collect them. You might also find bird bands or other tags once applied to animals or fish-types.

They will have numbers on them and sometimes provide a phone number as well.

You can do a great service by returning these to where it says to return. Also make notes of all information pertaining to the location of the find. This information may very well be the last resting place of that banded bird, so be correct in gathering it. For water detectors at the oceans, you may find crematory tags once provided with the ashes of loved ones who have past. These should not be returned unless to the crematory itself. People just don't like to be reminded about the event of casting those ashes at sea, and won't suspect that all of this will ever wash up on the coastline. Water detectors might find alligator, shark, or manatee tags. Your information will be used in tracking and mapping the creature's movement.

Finding and returning Class rings, one of the few rings with a vast amount of data provided, is also a great service. No other ring has this wealth of data and can be easy to return. Others can be harder because of their age. The good press will far outweigh the metal value when rendered down. Leave your business card when you return a ring and see if that doesn't create more leads.

Sometimes you will stumble on some real junk like syringes, dirty diapers, used rubbers, or crude weapons. These need to be disposed of properly and very carefully... just thought you might need to know.

J. Pierce metal detecting at a popular beach. Fresh water lake beaches are best when searched after a busy weekend.

Keep in mind that people will watch you where ever they see you. People are just curious, and you are fascinating to watch. You may be doing what they always wanted to do. So make a good impression. Make small holes, remove all trash and neatly fill all holes. When you notice your watcher, just smile and nod. Answer some questions, and try to go back to what you were doing. This might be a good time to drop your business card on a new prospect, and can get you to new leads.

When knocking on doors in an old neighborhood, wear work cloth, not dirty, worn-out items. Save these for dump digging or something else. Don't crowd the door and if more than one person wishes to search the site, only one should approach the door to ask permission. When dealing with older persons, talk slowly and ask- don't tell. When dealing with older people, most will be women, because they outlive the men, so be prepared to speak to a woman. Remove your hat and sunglasses, so she can see your eyes.

Or she won't trust you being in her yard, not to mention on her porch. She'll just want you gone. Be prepared to answer her questions of why would you be interested in hunting her yard. Offer to return any items she may know that are lost, or anything that may interest her. It may be a baby spoon or anything with a persons name on it. You never know till you've searched.

If you are lucky enough to research up a Civil War camp or site of any sort, you might have to offer a split with the owner of the property or, you may include the owner in the search party. It's his property after all, and they might not want anything at all.

You are an ambassador of metal detecting. People will form an opinion about you and all other detectorists. Help to make that a good opinion for all of us.

If you are planning a detecting trip to a location you may have researched, be sure to have a back-up site to fall back to, if for some reason site #1 is undetectable. This can save the outing if your first choice is closed to you. This becomes more important when a long drive and time is involved. Site #2 might just turn out to be the better choice anyway. I once traveled 80 miles to a lake site to search for five hours with little results....but the fishing was excellent and I had my fishing equipment. This saved the weekend because it became a fishing expedition.

Those are just some of my observations, by no means all that there is to metal detecting. You must read volumes on this subject and there is a ton of material available to the interested searcher.

Beginner treasure hunters should follow the styles and actions of experienced hunters and do nothing to attract unnecessary attention. This is done by going out early in the morning or during inclement weather. You will get more detecting time and less answering question time this way.

People do not need to know how successful you are. This can be serious trouble if you get the attention of the wrong type of people or the IRS. So precautions should be taken for privacy. This is a hobby, you're lucky to make expenses, you're in it for your health, you just love to irritate earthworms, and any of these expressions should be your response to the question "do you ever find anything with that thing?"

Avoid damaging sod or parks or even abandoned buildings. Replace and repair any and all signs of your activity. Of course, remove any trash you may have uncovered and leave the area in better condition than when you got there.

When working in abandoned buildings, houses or barns that may require limited trim removal (to inspect signals around baseboards and door frames), be sure to replace these items. If a discovery is made in a wall, door frame or stair tread, place a couple of steel or aluminum cans in it's place. This will tip-off any treasure hunter that may follow in your footsteps that the discovery was made. If you find cans or trash in this fashion, this is your tip-off that this area has been searched by another and to continue may be a waste of your time.

Chapter Three: Sluicing

Because this piece of equipment is so simple and easy to make, I can't believe I don't see them everywhere. Early prospectors made them out of ruff cut wood and covered the bottom with burlap. They mounted them on rockers (rocker boxes), made them short and made them a mile long to catch hydraulic run-off to catch the gold. So simple to make, they were left to rot when the prospector moved to new fields.

Anyone lucky enough to find one of these old, abandoned and rotting sluices will surely find gold in, around and under it, right where it lays. More thought on that later.

Sluices can sample a likely area for gold much faster than a gold pan because of the volume of material you can move over the same period of time. They will catch everything from flour gold to nuggets, coins and heavy relics.

Because of their size, a sluice can be carried easily in your car, ready to use anytime. If you are manufacturing your own sluice, why not make it fit your needs, for use or travel. Make it a two-piece, folding or, whatever. I experimented with different materials and settled on sheet metal and aluminum. I also fixed it so that I can change-out the mat quickly so my partner can clean one mat while I load-up another. This way, we know if we are finding color and adjust the material samples or move to somewhere else.

Remember, we are cheap. So make it out of items you have or can afford, and move up from there. Indoor carpet can catch a lot of gold. Shag carpet can be hard to clean. Remember, I'm cheap; I want the flour gold and black sands, to amalgamate after I have a large amount.

A sluice is quiet, only the sounds of the river can be heard. It can be used where a dredge (motors) is not allowed, sometimes due to fish hatch or other times restricted. If you have ever carried a camp and supplies into rugged Gold County, you know if you use a dredge it must be small. A sluice is lighter, easier and fits the bill for the tool to test your research.

Kids love to help with anything involving dirt, water and shovels, so you will have a lot of help with your operation if you choose to. Classify material through a half inch screen placed in the bottom of a bucket, which has the bottom cut out. Leave about half an inch of bottom to support the screen. Hey I'm cheap. Plus it stacks well with your normal buckets to handle your material, concentrates and camp duties. By the way, they say you can tell how good of a prospector someone is by the amount of buckets they carry, so carry a bunch to confuse any seasoned prospectors you may meet. These can be bought cheap at donut shops and bakeries.

Set-up in the river differs from location to location, river size and water speed. Generally, you want one inch of drop per running foot of sluice. Set-up your device by weighting it down with large rocks in the river, and slowly pour test material into the head (screen material of large rocks etc.). Material should wash through catching rocks at the back but most dirt washing out. You don't want it to sand up too much and rocks are hand picked out between pours. Before long you will instinctively set the correct angle and begin enjoying the fruits of your labor.

As for finding abandoned wooden sluices, place a large piece of plastic as close to the device as you can get it. Slowly move the sluice onto the sheeting and begin to take it apart. The sides can hold a great deal of fine gold, black sand and flow sands.

The riffles can have the same things and maybe more. Carefully take the whole device apart, saving all sand

and gravel and pan this later at the river. Now you'll need to detect the area in which it was laying and scoop signals into a gold pan to locate. Also remember to clean the burlap material that might line the bottom and any rags used to fill gaps in the sides or to stop leaks. All of this will catch flour gold and sands and need to be panned out to find values.

This is just a light touch on the subject and large volumes are printed on this subject and also need to be studied.

Happy Prospecting.

Treasure Hunting takes time and effort......to keep it interesting and profitable.

Chapter Four: Dredging

Everyone knows that dredges have revolutionalized prospecting. The sheer volume of material that can be moved by one or two people is an immense advantage over the earliest prospector. Back then, prospectors were lucky if they could effectively move more than one cubic yard. Today, a simple 2 inch dredge will move that amount in one hour. A three inch will double that and, a four inch will double that amount. You can imagine what a 8 inch or 10 inch device will move. With that kind of volume, today's prospector can collect gold in smaller values and still make it pay over time in areas that were abandoned by early prospectors. Add to this, the air compressors and flush hoses that allow us to get the gold that is normally hard to find. Research mining claim records for claims that were abandoned and check out the possibilities. Only a few states in the lower 48 do not have gold in some quantity. The first US Mints were in North Carolina and Georgia because of the volume of gold there. There are many great books just on this subject, and if this is your niche, read them.

So…What about those of us who do not live near the mother load? Fear not. We can use this same technology to vacuum swimming holes, low water crossings, rope swings, and any other place where people have gathered. The fact that people have lost items in the water is well documented. And, because it was once lost in the water is exactly why it is still there to be discovered. Military camps, battle sites, and forts fit this bill too, because they mostly had to be set-up near the water. Everyday a detail would have the responsibility of getting water for the fort. This water source would also be used for bathing and washing clothing. And, what was once a source of water for washing and survival is now a source for lost valuables.

The dredge works so well because it allows you to spend less time recovering your target by simply sucking it from the bottom. The denser, more valuable metal generally stays in the top part of the dredge, while lighter items end up in the bottom section. By adding a section in the bottom of the dredge with holes in it or screen, you keep it from loading up with dirt and sand, or small pebbles. This allows for longer periods of searching between clean-ups because the dredge won't load up as much.

It is a good idea to keep all the junk and trash items you find so you don't keep detecting the same junk. The glass, fishing lures, pull tabs, cut-up aluminum cans and bottle caps that find their way to your trash bucket will befriend you to any authority figure that may be curious of your activity.

I once had a sheriff show up where I was detecting, a park swimming area used for many years. I was just using a detector, floating screen and shovel, so I wasn't making a lot of noise or mudding the water. He asked me what I was doing and I explained. He seemed jumpy till I showed him the coins and common items in my apron. Then I showed him a double-handful of trash and glass and he was smiles all over. I was just some harmless nut in the water gathering junk. When I left for home that day I had 3 gold bands, 2 were 14K, 2 silver rings, $6.50 in change and, oh yeah, the junk. He waves at me when he sees me now, from his car.

Always check local or state laws or restrictions, and always get permission where possible. Many Park Ranger types take notice of the cloudy water you might stir-up, so be aware of this. Most officials will love the fact that you are cleaning up the waterway. Where I operate in a moving stream, the bottom cleans up nicely and looks better than before I got there.

An example of a larger coin dredge made portable by using heavy duty inter-tubes.

Another operation is to use a hookah air and weight belt and search deep under dive platforms and floating platforms, or rope swings. Here Visibility is at it's worst and you'll stir-up slit, so "find and vac" works best. Find the target with the detector and vacuum on it till it disappears up the hose.

You can hear the signal go up the hose if you hold the search coil next to it. In this type of work, it is best to have a tender on the dredge because you will be too far away to monitor it. You will want to use an underwater light also.

As in the case above, you will want to replace to metal nozzle on the hose with PVC so as not to interfere with the underwater detector. You can also add an electrical sweep 45 degree angle so placement and pick-up of targets is easier. Use enough weight to keep you on the bottom. Using a dive watch, you could keep track of your time. You need to know how long a tank of gas lasts on your equipment. You may want to tie a goody bag onto the hose near the slobber end so you can place all the garbage and goodies you find in it. No need to send them to the surface operation if you remove them from the nozzle. That is where I keep a light till I need it.

It would be advisable to obtain a wet suit for these dives because you will be at it for some time. Longer than with compressed air because of the hookah. You'll be surprised at how fast time passes and the dredge will possibly run out of gas before you are ready to come up.

As you can see, this type of endeavor requires more equipment which also means more cost. And it also means you have to spend more time at doing it. You also may have to take on a partner, which creates timing problems- because you just can't grab your beeper and go.

But ....

Maybe this should have been the last chapter because this is where I've ended up after 20 plus years of TH'ing. It's hard to keep this secret and has to be explained as part of Gold Prospecting.

Bob Smith has written an excellent book, *Coin and Relic Dredging*. I wish I had read this before I began building my first outfit, because he explains how he modified a gold dredge into a coin dredge that works with his detector. It has become one of my "25 Essential Books for the Well-read Treasure Hunter" List, and I highly recommend adding it to your personal library. Mr. Smith is a very motivated treasure hunter and has some very good ideas.

Sniping

Gold sniping, on the other hand, takes little more than a good mask and snorkel, old tennis shoes and some of the same tools you used to dig bottle dumps. Your large screwdriver, garden trowel, small spoon, large tweezers, and a ping pong paddle will just about cover your tool list. A wet suit is useful because of the exposure to water over time. Bearing streams tend to be the snow melt runoff type and are cold. A rugged bowl or gold pan is helpful to carry your tools and to bring material from the creek bottom.

I like to use those little rubber bulb snot suckers, so unmercifully used on infants, to blow sand and material out of cracks and seams.

You'll have to be selective about your locations because here you need bedrock and hard pack to be exposed, or you'll have to move overburden. You can fan with your paddle but can't expect to move tons of cover that way. A swift stream or river works best, as well as a bright, overhead sun to light-up the gold caught in cracks or crevasses and other traps in the bedrock.

Pill bottles with flip tops work well to stow your finds and you can collect gravel and fine sand from any traps in a plastic gold pan to pan out later. Pry bars and large screwdrivers are recommended to break into large cracks because they hold those bigger nuggets and lots of fine color.

This cheap and quiet, as well as relaxing way to prospect for gold has long been a slow favorite. It works best after storms or floods and can quickly tell you the amount of value in an area new to you. And again, this is something that the whole family can do. You might be surprised who finds the gold.

Dredging in Northern Calif. in 1986 with friend Andy Rizzo, using a two inch backpack dredge.

My son Justin, setting-up a 3-inch coin dredge w/ compressed air. Notice the Dam that forms this swimming area is not flowing. Lower water levels help "TH'ing" more areas.

"Today is the Day!!" Mel Fisher

Chapter Five: Beachcombing

Just the mention of this word fills my head with the visions of ghostly wrecks, sea salt spray, huge expanses of sandy beaches, wheeling seabirds, foamy surf and blue skies as far as the eye can see. An adventure in the offering, to whom ever would take the steps to that direction. I feel sorry for those who have never experienced bare feet in the sand and surf.

The beach is where the ocean cleanses herself of all of her dead and man's wonton invasion. Sometimes it takes time to wash it out of her system- but she (the ocean) will eventually get it out. Walk the beach at first light and be amazed at the amount of flotsam and debris on the beach. Glass net floats to refrigerators. Butane bottles to car parts and everything in between. Shells, starfish and horseshoe crabs fill in the gaps in-between the man-made items. Large timbers and telephone poles wash-up too, anything is possible.

An extremely valuable coastal treasure is Ambergris. It is used to stabilize fragrances in the making of perfume, and it is valued as high as $5000 per pound.

The color is usually grayish, a yellowish green, or olive blue. Its texture will also run the spectrum, from spongy soft (like a piece of fat) to hard rosin. As for its origin, Ambergris is formed in the stomach of whales. Because whales travel so extensively, and the oceans are in constant movement, Ambergris can wash up anywhere. It can also remain unnoticed for a long time. It is left and reclaimed by the ocean in the next storm. Because of this it might appear as a waxy disk mixed in with other flotsam and trash along the beach.

Sea shells should never be viewed as something of little value. Even well-worn scallop shells make nice wind chimes. Many shells on Florida and Texas coasts fetch a high price. An example would be Sanibel, Florida, which is highly touted for its precious shells. Every spring, collectors, dealers and the like, flock to the island's shell fair. My family vacationed there when I was growing up. On the trip there, or on the way home, we would stop and visit the shell factory. It was huge then, similar to the size of Wal-Mart stores today. I have never seen so many shells, in one place, in my life. I can only imagine what it is like now, so many years late, as well as the values of those early found treasures of the sea.

I know most of you adventurous types know about beachcombing. But, what about lake beaches close to your area? In the early morning hours, you have the same opportunity to find items lost during the night or over the period of a couple of days, like after Holidays and weekends. I water detect a couple of lake beaches, and get there at first light. After a weekend, the beach area is covered with aluminum cans and bottles of all kinds. Sometimes you'll find clothing and lawn chairs, toys and swim gear. A couple of elderly gentlemen (because I like them) also get there at first light and pick all of this up. I've seen them with two large garbage bags full of aluminum cans daily. They also pick-up all of the trash and dispose of it in the nearby trashcans

They never complain and seldom miss an opportunity to say hello or wave, and tote their treasures back to their auto trunks.

Where ever you live, there is a place where people swim and party during the summer and holidays. When they do, they leave items behind, trash and treasure. Some of us can see the treasure in the trash.

Many well known names come to mind as great Treasure Hunters along the coast, Mel Fisher, Kip Wagner, Art McKee, and Robert Marx. Kip Wagner kicked off his career as a TH'er after finding oxidized pieces of eight near

Sebastian Inlet. Research lead him to venture farther out and find the vessels that deposited this Treasure. Remember, cost of funding such a venture is extremely high and many have failed- even after raising venture capital.

There is really no way of truly knowing how many other lucky strollers along the beach found valuable gold and silver items from these same wrecks. How many small fortunes have gone unpublished or unannounced? I dare guess more than a few. The really successful Treasure Hunters rarely publicize their finds, thus insuring future successes. Otherwise, they will have numerous people and entities scurrying-over their site, trying to pick up something or maybe everything-which has been the case when Governments get involved.

This is not a beach necessarily, but Colleges have annual Bonfires or homecoming rallies (also High schools), where people lose items in a known area, generally at night. I found a location once used many years ago. It turned out to be a silver mine of coins, and I highly recommend this type of location.

Outdoor concerts are in this category and also need to be hunted at first light the morning after. Expect to find the unexpected.

These sites are advertised in the Newspaper and only need the minimal planning to search. It may boil-down to: who gets there first- for the early bird gets the worm.

Seek what you enjoy....Enjoy what you seek.

Chapter Six: Areas Flooded or Damaged By Water

Flood waters always erode tons of earth and, almost all rivers and streams flood at one time or another. Most actually flood every spring. Rivers change their coarse completely after flooding. Some are completely different than they were one hundred years ago. Even the Mighty Mississippi River is this way. A paddlewheel that once plied the river course was found 30 feet deep in a corn field several years back. After numerous attempts it was finally excavated by the owner of the property. It was a Time Capsule of early trade goods and food stuffs, preserved as it was when this vessel sank. This by and large, is due to the lack of air and preserving quality of the mud. Just because this project was on land and not water, did not make it any less remarkable as a recovery. But by the persistence of those involved, did it get completed.

This case is modern compared to the Northern Seaboard's history, or that of Europe, or that for the Far East. All have great hidden wealth in their living waterways.

After heavy rains are over, I walk all known water hazards and waterways looking for erosion. Let Mother Nature do the work of removing and exposing items of interest for you. Many bottle dumps and old homesteads have been found this way.

A good hint of a homestead or dump are bits of broken glass and rotted cans, red brick, oyster shells, and bits of tile. Anything man made should be investigated. It helps to know your area's history as well.

In areas known to have Gold, watch for exposed hard packs in ditches and draws. Under and behind any rock or obstacles is a place to look for small placer gold. Remember the winter storms of 1986 in California? Flooding in

Placerville created a new gold rush when word got out that people were finding gold in the streets. People were actually picking gold flakes out of the expansion joints where curbing and drains were joined. You know, that ½ inch or ¾ inch piece of tar impregnated fiber providing separation for expansion in the curb. People sat in their yards (and the yards of others) and picked flakes out with tweezers form this manmade long tom that runs through every city and town of America. If you ever find a culvert going under the road, check the first few ribs (riffles?) on the uphill side. I hear of a guy who searches all of them he can find in Gold Country. Some of them are large enough to walk into.

Again, erosion is a powerful force and can eat giant scares and channels may expose regions not before seen. Doing this in gold country may just uncover new gold discoveries.

A long time swimming and boating area that is now low and dry because of drought condition. This is a great place to sift the soil to remove junk and retrieve goodies before using a metal detector.

This is the same swimming and boating area many years ago. This photo was found during research at a local college library.

Just another day metal detecting, I just happened to find another coin for the log books.

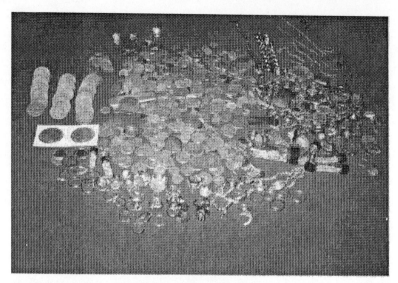

Over time, your collection of lost valuables can accumulate. Everything from coins to rings and necklaces is out there, waiting to be discovered.

An example of some of the more unique items you might find, including: bullets, badges, old toys, keys and all sorts of other goodies.

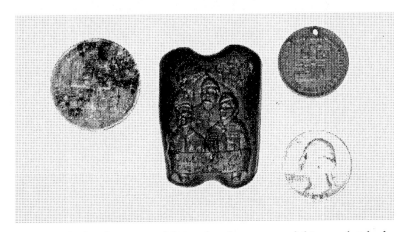

If you look closely at two of the trade tokens, you might see what looks like a German swastika. But in this case, you would be mistaken. The coins actually predate the Holocaust and the swastika symbol means good luck. Hitler stole it, and has given it a bad cogitation ever since.

Bottles like these are very collectable, and a good place to find them is in attics.

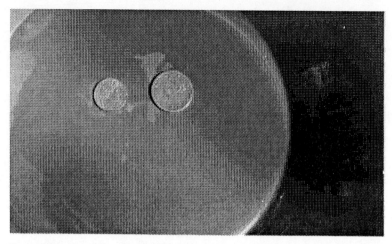

Two coins from the same period, from two different countries- an U.S. $10 gold piece and a French Franc. The types of coins found in old mining camps or early logging camps. The abundance of gold in California only added to the high numbers of gold coins in circulation in the West. Some of these gold coins were minted by private assayers to help trade in the area, a few of these turn-up today for treasure hunters.

Gold still can be found in no less than fourteen of the lower 48 states. It's most beautiful in its' natural state, and was also used in trade in this form.

Cache hunting is one of the greatest forms of treasure hunting. Most of the hidden cashes will be small in size but great in value. Most are the results of years of savings and hiding money. This hide was only $25.05 in face value with seven foreign silver coins, two U.S. Half dimes and two shield nickels, as well as two early U.S. silver dollars.

Always search a well put together wood pile for hidden cache.

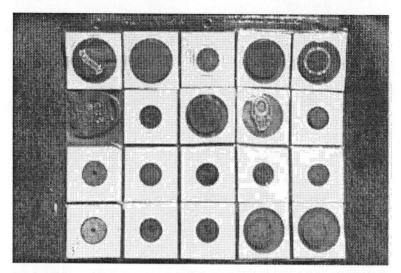

Items found are not always identifiable coins; some are advertisement tokens, tax and transportation tokens or political tokens. Each of these categories is an area of specialized collectors. Most of these types of tokens have a much lower production run when compared to coin mintage.

This small 14K ring is a nice addition to any collection and a nice sight in the bottom of the scoop. This scoop is a stainless steel long- handled type and shows very little wear even with a years use.

Over time and with normal activity, the hobbyist metal detector can amass a notable collection of silver items. Most items found will have been out of circulation, some for many years. What better way to get started in coin collecting?

Many different and unusual items found while metal detecting- some typical and others non-typical.

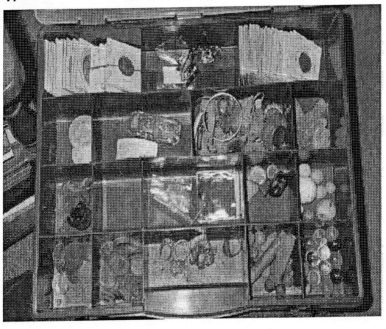

This is a GPAA outing in Pine Log CA. in September of 2000. Pictured are a 6 inch triple-slice dredge and a 3 inch high banker in the background. This lease has two 6 inch and two 4 inch triples and two 3 inch high backers working all day for a week. This is the best way for a serious gold seeker to find the gold, and develop skills. The water is crystal clear and cold.

Gold dredging in Gold Country around Redding Calif. with 2 inch Gold Bug unit.

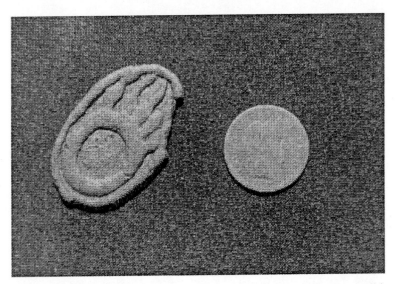

An example of a Barber dime with an early piece of silver, possible Wampum.

Chapter Seven: Treasure in Attics, Garages, Storerooms and Basements.

Most people realize there can be tremendous amounts of treasure in attics and basements, lying dormant since placed there years ago. Things like baseball cards, movie posters, old furniture, appliances, old toys and antique clothing, old dishes, bottles, marbles, old newspapers, arrowheads, trunks full of records, postcards and letters from loved ones away to war are just some of the interesting things that can be found in attics. The list goes on and on. But how do some people get lucky and find these treasures, while most people don't?

It's because some people are more persistent and they make themselves available to find these items. They even get paid to clean-out and carry-off such treasures! They place handyman and haul-off Ads in local newspapers and look for opportunities to help clean-out old places after deaths or illness. Sometimes it's just cleaning up a property to sell.

They may work hard all summer hauling away true junk and rubbish to get that one call to clean out a collapsing garage before demolition. Maybe the call is to haul away a whole attic full of "stuff" so that the home owner can turn the attic into another bedroom. The reasons are as numerous as the treasure.

The greatest part is that this could be your new part-time job, and people could pay you to get rid of their trash. Many times people will get rid of their own trash and the landfill will claim it-forever. And, like any job, you have costs like fuel and dump fees, so be sure to keep this in mind when setting your charges.

If you find something truly valuable, you may want to pay something to the former owner or donate something to a wonderful cause. That is up to you, but this new problem is better than your old problem, the money problem.

We once found hundreds of glass Mason quart canning jars, with food still in them. We offered the owner something for them- they were just happy to be rid of them. We had to dispose of who-knows-how-much bad food in order to clean the quart jars. It seemed like it took a long time to do. But we did it, and it was wonderful.

This kind of work can be an adventure in itself sometimes. Watch out for wild animals living in abandoned outbuildings. Bee's and wasps love long unused buildings and even attics. Once these critters get established, they can be extremely hard to remove. If you find this situation, back off and research the possible fixes, then move accordingly.

Treasure hunters must set goals and know what they are after. Everything has value somewhere. Maintain a treasure attitude and a commitment to salvaging anything of value in all situations.

This is the Land of Hopes and Dreams

Chapter Eight: Research

This seems like a good time to mention research. No self respecting author has ever left this subject out of any How-to book on TH'ing and I won't be the first- in this area anyway.

Something that has set the successful Treasure Hunter apart from the rest of the pack is his dedication, imagination, determination and his working knowledge, but research is the keystone for his continual success. He has a Treasure attitude, a focus in his daily life, and the information is readily available, waiting for his appraisal and collection. It's in the archives of the daily newspaper. Tons of information lies in every Library in the country. Every official building downtown has old maps of their areas of interest in drawers or hanging on the walls. The Court House, Tax Assessor Office, Surveys and City Development office all have vast collections of local information. Old photos of your area of interest are a huge asset; it's like viewing an area as it was years ago.

A good starting point would be your local Highway Department. Obtain County highway maps of your area and of those surrounding your County. Then transfer all other information you collect from older maps, USGS maps, aerial photographs, the GPAA catalog, Railroad surveys, and treasure publications onto these maps. This will help by showing you what roads (paved, gravel, dirt, unimproved etc.) you can use to travel to your site. You can color code areas of interest or assign sites a number by importance. For example, #1 best, #2 good, #3 lesser and so on. When planning a trip to search a site, always have a close-by backup or contingency target. If for some reason you can not search site #1, you'll have a fallback site to hunt.

These Highway maps cost 50 cents a piece in my state, so if I mess one up or want to change the way I mark them, I can afford another. I also add comments in the margins of source materials and you would not want to do this to an old map. Keep all of your source materials safe in files and your composite maps with you. Continually add new information you find about Forts, lost mines, water crossings, Ferry crossings, ghost towns, battles, camps, stagecoach stops.... the list is endless, to this map. Pretty soon you'll have an all purpose treasure map of your own making from your research.

The computer and the hundreds of Web sites it offers are by far the greatest research tool available to the modern Treasure Hunter. It is unbelievable how much information is out there waiting for you to use it. Universities have map sites (check out University of Texas Collection) and archives of data. Museums have Web sites. Most all government entities have a Web site. All of the great Treasure Hunters have their own Web sites, with tons of information for free and for sale. All of the treasure publications also have web sites with daily updates, stories and how-to tips. This is the information era on the info highway! You may find too much data and have a hard time stopping to do actual searching. Your new problem becomes data management and sorting of all your new found materials. I use files in a file cabinet and a bookshelf.

I've found so much data, of regions and areas not close-by that, I had to limit the information that I viewed. I did gather maps, charts and GPS locations of known wrecks, and other data for my brother in Florida- just in case we get back to the "Gold Coast".

No matter how you slice it, information is knowledge, knowledge is power. It allows you an edge over the competition, no matter how persistent. Use it to your advantage.

If you do have a computer, you most likely have a printer. When you do find those pearls of wisdom, print them. The reason is because you may never be able to find this source site again. I've copied domains, addresses; you name it and sometimes can't get that information back. Sometimes you'll start at one place and link over four or five times, and find an unknown jewel, only to be lost to cyberspace.

Good old fashion Library books about your local history have information that directly applies to your area. Search reference materials on reserve and copy important items. Many are authored by Historic Societies or local Historians and can cover subjects about Courthouses, old schools, churches, picnics, holiday celebrations, circuses, and tent revivals.

Focus on events and documented happenings in your community- the older the event the better. What were the leisure activities of the earliest inhabitants? Where did they hold the few celebrations they had, and what were the holidays or social interest? Was the town formed around the railroad, forts, or commerce? Did it have water crossings, floods or droughts? You get the idea. Figure these questions out and the new questions you now have uncovered and you'll have some respectable research folders.

Check your local Historical societies and if you are really lucky, check your local college or university. They receive personal diaries, letters, and journals of the areas prominent citizenry. The most prominent residents of the community may have a different viewpoint than you do today. They also have huge databases of early activities and micro film storage. This is an excellent source for historic information.

Remember all of the persistent people who stopped you with questions while you were detecting? Have they asked, "Do you really find stuff with that thing?" How have you answered that question? The answer differs from time to time and person to person, of course. Why not ask our own questions. Senior citizens have a wealth of memories of your area, and they also have the time to tell you about them.

They engaged you with questions first, so what do you have to lose? They already know you are interested in metal detecting so that barrier has been breeched. Be sure to add their information to your search list, regardless of how far fetched it may sound. Later research may very well confirm all they have already told you.

MAPS

Maps are the single most important research source you will ever find for Treasure Hunting. City maps, Railroad maps, survey maps, highway maps, and very detailed Plat maps are just an example of a few. Every one of your local agencies have their own maps. Trust me; they do have old maps too. As I said earlier, transpose all other map data on to a county highway map, so you will know how to get to the search site once you've discovered its location.

Gravity carries all loose objects to the Earth and holds them there till they are forced from her grip. Every site you can think of is inherently old, but not necessarily productive for the Treasure Hunter.

Under all things is the Earth. It was here long before mankind walked upon it, and it will be here long after you and I are gone.

Unless it was inhabited or had a use that drew people, it was a chunk of land that held the earth together. By expanding our knowledge and research, we will find the productive areas and profit if possible.

Chapter Nine: Water Detecting

If you haven't noticed yet, this is my single most enjoyable activity, outside of chasing my wife, and I may have chased her with my underwater detector once before. I first read some articles about converting a land detector to hunt in the water, back in 1984 or there bouts. And being the adventurous type (another word for being silly), I jumped on the idea with both feet. I built a floating screen and a float for the detector and everything else that I could build. I bought a cheap scoop that might have worked in the soft sands of Florida, but not in my area. All coils in those days were hollow and floated badly. Following the advice of the articles, I assembled my floating-water unit and beat-feet it to the nearest lake. That first outing wasn't too successful, mostly a test run.

The second trip was not much better, but I stayed at it. Being a certified Diver, it was difficult not to get totally in there. The hard gravel rock bottom was especially bad. The scoop that I had bought didn't hold up at all, a side-effect of being cheap. What little I did find didn't come close to repairing my detector and I never went back into the water.

Years past and kids became my main interest. Living got in the way. Eventually, I returned to land detecting once I no longer was so busy. Now it was harder to find much at all at any of my old haunts, because everyone else had kept on detecting and new folks entered the field. Finds were thin unless I found a virgin site (research), and I became very good at developing these types of leads.

Once while detecting a beach at a local lake, I wondered into the water, very shallow of course, without jeopardizing my hip mounted detector.

I stood in little more then 10 inches of water and had targets everywhere. Recovery was a problem, but I was finding good items and a good number of them. So I recreated my floating screen and modified a #2 shovel with a 2 inch steel strap welded across the back and hammered the middle out to resemble a spoon. The only problem was staying shallow and working stooped-over to handle the screen. This, of course, lead to more research work. I began researching water recreation areas no longer popular and out of use. The drought added to my success by lowering the water levels and exposing new areas to search through the summer. The quality of the finds were remarkable, with a high number of gold and silver jewelry.

With the promise of rainfall during the Fall and Winter, I decided to make the move to the next step, an underwater detector and move into the deeper water. Wow. It was unbelievable; the fifth target I found was a gold ring! In perspective it was a great day. It stayed that way the rest of the year. At one beach, I found 5 gold rings in one day (and 5 silver) and 3 gold rings (4 silver) the next. I found coins by the handfuls with a large number of larger denomination coins.

The best part is that the competition is still on the beach and hasn't gotten into the water yet. In the past 16 months I have not seen another water detector in my area. I know there's one out there, I just haven't met him. The swimming areas have a chance to accumulate items, sometimes on top of each other. Unlike dry land, items lost in the water stay in the water with little chance of being recovered. This happens year after year, in some cases, many years. Don't get me wrong- there is a ton of junk lost or discarded in the water also. But even this can be rewarding in those older recreation areas. I've found brass whistles, brass safety pins, lead soldiers, old hot wheels and tootsie toys, marbles, and old sunglasses.

Using a 3-inch dredge and under-water detector to vacuum the bottom of a once popular swimming area

I've found an enormous amount of lead fishing weights (reusable as fishing weights or capable of being melted down) and an antique fly fishing reel, as well as old lures. Mostly there are pull-tabs and ring-tabs and other items that emit a signal similar to that of gold.

You must use no discrimination, dig all signals, and keep all junk. But as I've said before, the really great objects are to be found in the second layer and below, under the trash. The amount of broken glass amazes me, and the large items baffle me. I've even found a iron closing/opening handle from an eighteen inch gate valve, which I sand blasted and painted. All of this was found just wading into chest deep water with an underwater detector and later, a stainless steel scoop.

Once these old haunts began to become short of targets, I adapted the dredge with hooka for coin hunting (see chapter Four).This expanded the search area to deep water, under rope swings, slides and diving boards. Each year, these locations are restocked and the process begins again.

For equipment, form follows function. You will need a sturdy floating screen and a rugged recovery tool, the cheaper the better. I cut the top five inches from a sturdy Styrofoam cooler that was used to ship frozen meats or something. Cut and work into a square shape ½" screen or hardware cloth, leaving about an inch of space at the bottom. This should look like a basket. In one corner you may want to add a small piece of ¼" mesh to catch the very small items that will be recovered. Small ear rings, 22 bullets and casings, brass rivets from blue jeans and similar items will stay in this mesh and keep you from digging them up over and over. Tie a small cord to the float to secure it to yourself and you won't need to hold on to it.

Scoops can be as different as the different areas of America. In soft sandy areas you can use thin lightweight screen scoops; in others you may need rugged stainless steel scoops. If the bottoms of your area waterways are rocky, you might what to use a #2 shovel with some modifications. Beat the middle rib out a little to give it the shape of a spoon and weld a 2 inch steel strap across the back to hold more material and improve the area you step on to dig detected items. The best thing about a shovel-scoop is that they are cheap and you possibly already have one. You will also like the fact that the wooden handle floats, making it easier to keep track of.

When I travel to a new area to search, I always take all of my different tools and scoops, this way I can select the proper tool to work that site more efficiently. You have heard the right tool for the job? It applies here.

Always wear shoes of some sort when going into the water. Cheap shoes with Velcro closures work best, because there is no metal to interfere with the detector. Get shoes several sizes too large so that they fit better over waders or neoprene booties. Looks are not important here ladies.

After locating a target, pinpoint it, and then place your foot next to the coil. Note where the target might be in relation to your foot (toe, instep or heel), move the coil well out of the area and place the scoop beside your foot and behind the target. Depending on how deep you think the target is, scoop shallow, medium or deep to recover the item. With practice you'll have most targets recovered on the first try. The worst targets are the multiple coin drop area because they are so close and so many signals that it will be hard to pinpoint one at a time. But, you'll love the returns on this type of signal.

Use waders or a wetsuit if you want to get really deep. This will allow you to stay in the water for longer periods of time and protect you from scrape from underwater obstacles. This is very important when searching saltwater regions. I feel more secure when hunting in new areas with a wetsuit, until I know what the bottom is like and if it is level and without holes or drop offs.

Keep the detector coil in contact with the bottom so you will "feel" any holes or drop offs before you step into it. This is most important if you have converted a dry land detector to use in the water or are wearing waders. Be careful not to breach the top of your waders, or they will fill with water and this is dangerous.

I could go on and on about this type of detecting, but the best advice is to try it, develop a style and form that works for you. I'm just happy to belly-button deep in the water, any water. But add to that a couple of gold rings, and I just get happier.

Swimming Areas:

Swimming area means swimming holes, not just beaches, on rivers, lakes, creeks, stock tanks and ponds. It will most likely always be water deep enough to dive into, may offer shade and might have a rope swing. This swing may move around too, as the trees become damaged and limbs break. I see this more often than not.

The deep holes are where the best items are found, but only for the specialist with scuba, dredge and underwater detector. The shallow water detector can get close to these areas, and if you are the first to detect here, you may be surprised at the amount of coins and jewelry. This same fellow can chase the receding water during droughts and improve his chances. I can no longer be content to hunt the beach and must search the water because of the values found there and the lack of competition.

Now the bad news, this specialty requires the right equipment to be successful and that always cost more. Many attempts have been made to covert land detectors for use in the water with mixed results. Waist deep in the water is a bad place to have an accident with your expensive detector built for land use. The other bad news, while digging abundant good targets, you will dig quite a bit of trash. The need to use little or no discrimination shouldn't need to be stated....for the remarkable number of gold items found in swimming areas.

The first swimming area that I searched, a roped-off designated swimming area, turned up 3 gold rings the second day that I hunted it. The first day there I found 8 nickels, 2 silver rings, 3 junk rings and two fist fulls of trash- bummer. But, why all the nickels? That's why I went back.

A normal, quiet morning in a popular swimming beach.
What better way to spend few early morning hours?

The third day I found 5 gold rings (some with small diamonds), 12 Nickels, some silver and a ton of trash items. I continued to work this area all summer and fall. Now I need to wait for this "Bank" to be redeposited during swim season, but there is little junk there to be found. And if the person who hunted the area before me returns, he'll soon leave thinking he found everything the first time. He obviously used discrimination the entire time he searched and didn't want to dig the trash. You will dig trash and pull tabs if you want to be successful at Treasure Hunting.

We all have heard wonderful stories of gold Spanish doubloons and silver pieces-of-eight washing up on coastal beaches all along America. They are true-for those lucky enough to be at the right place at the right time. Hurricane treasure was deposited during a hurricane and it needs a hurricane to uncover it.

Otherwise those goodies are buried under 6 to 12 feet of sand. Loose, light sand and shell have little chance of holding valuable heavy metals in place and they will sink until something stops them, like clay, hard pack or artificial bedrock. These valuables also have had 220 to 300 years to sink and move around.

The best time to search would be immediately after a large storm. The successful Treasure Hunter won't wait that long. Research must be done before hand and this data saved to use at the right time.

The beach still has newly deposited treasures and coins to be found. To improve your chances of success, visit your target beach during peak times and record crowd placement and note activities on the beach. If you'll have the opportunity to hunt here over a period of time, mark pier pilings, rocks or any objects that are permanent fixtures on the beach. This way you'll know if the sand is being deposited or removed from the area. You'll get more detecting depth with the sand removal, so seek out this condition. You may just find some previously out of reach treasure here. Erosion is your best friend at the beach. Allow natural forces to remove material and seek out this activity.

Spring Break is your second-best friend at the beach. College youth swarm and pack popular beaches for a very short period and can get pretty wild. Why not park your camp-set right in the middle of this throng and plan to detect during the night while the revelers have moved their parties to town? If you noted where the masses were the thickest, you should have the best results there.

Metal detectors have been around long enough now that we can almost safely assume you aren't the first person to hunt a site that is visible to the public.

Be the first to a producing site, and the best detector operator to work the site, and you will do the best job at liberating its treasure.

Boat Ramps, Boat Launching Areas and Mooring Areas:

Boat ramps in dry and arid regions can be accessible to most anyone with a detector. Docks and marina slips are a different story. Like all other water activities, slippery hands lose objects that can't be recovered. This inaccessibility is your chance for retrieval. You may be able to run a part time business recovering lost items.

Be careful what you call junk before you discard your trash items. An old set of keys in conglomerate (Steel, brass, and silver electrolyzed together) will look bad until you clean and break the different elements. I recently found a very old set of keys that had a Mexican Peso drilled and placed on the steel key ring. Older watches are very collectable and can be found in numbers around docks. For some reason, people toss their wedding bands from docks when they are through with them. I don't know why, but I don't mind.

Never stop learning, never stop improving.

Chapter Ten: Used Equipment

As you move from one interest to another, you may find the need for another type of equipment or the need to sell some of your present equipment.

Hopefully, you've started with the bare basics and have financed all of your advancements with the treasure you've recovered. More importantly, you've obtained equipment at a discount or second hand.

Many people have purchased equipment in the pursuit of Treasure Hunting with an unreal expectation of returns, grand quest and rewards without the necessary labor. They simply allow themselves to become lackadaisical about their pursuit and their equipment languishes in the garage or nearest closet. Others under estimated their own limitations or over spent too soon in the game.

Many people must sell good little used equipment because of health problems. They waited too long to enjoy this as a leisure activity and no longer have the stamina or motivation to continue.

The venues offering used Treasure Hunting equipment are a veritable smorgasbord. Local and regional newspapers are a good starting point. Treasure magazines are a logical next step. The benefit with them is the wealth of information available by association. Today every published magazine has its own Website, offering huge volumes of information.

This brings me to probably the best place to find new and used equipment, the website bulletin board.

They are too numerous to mention, but I will mention a few,

www.losttreasure.com
www.icmj.com

www.unitedprospectors.com

www.goldledge.com

www.bertaut.com/treasurelinks

These all have free listings for 30 to 60 days and unite many a buyer and seller. For example, I needed a larger dredge with an air compressor to convert into a coin dredge to access the deeper water. I posted a simple want ad stating my interest in a 2 inch, 2 1/2 inch, or 3 inch dredge w/ air. I received four replies to those ads in the first week, before I could make-up my mind, I had four more responses. Within three weeks I had a wonderful 3 inch Keene with T80 compressor and high bank assembly and extras. The computer makes responding to offers and communicating back and forth cheap and easy.

Almost all of the Treasure magazines have an ad section in the back as well. The California Mining Journal has one of the best ad sections, if you can't find what you are looking for there, access their website.

Once you begin looking around, you will be amazed at the amount of used and serviceable equipment that is available. Camping equipment will be found in abundance this way. Many foreword thinking individuals laid-in equipment from AC/DC generator sets to freeze dried foods, from kerosene lamps to composting toilets for Y2K. Many had to sell some of these items off to recoup some of their money, some are still letting go of some of the equipment as their children grow up and they need the money to send them into the world. Hopefully, they are a little wiser of the possible failures and how to survive by themselves.

Swap meets and flea markets will rarely have mainstream mining equipment, but will offer different items that you need. You can find yard and garden tools, hand tools useful to mining and 5 gal. buckets. Or, how about ping pong paddles? Some divers use these to fan sand and overburden to find treasure with or without a water detector.

They work great and you usually find them in pairs. This is also a great place to sell your equipment, items or finds.

I sold the first dredge I ever owned by answering a want ad in the local newspaper, local as in Central Texas, where there is no gold. He was buying everything he could find and I sent him to a friend of mine with many more items. I wish I still had that little 2 inch 2 cycle dredge.

The point is, equipment of all sorts can be found everywhere. You can scourge items together and not really have to scrimp. Save your real purchase power for technology and performance. Once you begin your adventure, you will think of items you have seen but didn't get, now seeing a use for it, you'll watch for another.

You have a better chance to succeed if your equipment pays for itself and you feel as if your investment is bringing a return. Less expensive equipment fills the bill, and you may be more likely to allow family and friends to use your equipment and develop into your own small network.

EBay

This is such a part of my daily life that I seem to take it for granted. It has to be the single most important auction house in the cyber community today. It is practical as it is versatile, offering everything from antiques to zambonies. I visit this site almost daily and have half a dozen favorite categories devoted to treasure.

This is a great place to get literature concerning your interests also. Many of my research books came from this resource.

EBay is possibly the premier venue to sell your items as well. The price you ultimately receive (or pay) for your item may be less than you could have gotten from a collector of such item, but it is more likely you'll have more interested individuals concentrated in one place and receive a fair price.

The continuous nature of eBay adds to the likelihood of you selling your treasures.

I see this venue only getting better as time goes on, its stock has gone up in a down economy, and there must be a reason for that. All of my trading experiences have been good ones, but you are welcomed to draw your own conclusions.

Poor man wants to be rich

Rich man wants to be King

Kings ain't satisfied, he wants everything.

Bruce Springsteen

Chapter Eleven: Advertise Your Interest

When doing your research, you will find that people, friends and family are a wealth of information. How will you ever know this information if they aren't compelled to tell you? Why not advertise your interest and what it is that you do? Some metal detectorist never let their friends or co-workers know what it is that drives them. You may be surprised at the amount of quality data that they might know, or they may want you to hunt their property. This sometimes is all it takes to begin detecting an older established neighborhood.

Simple light conversation works well, if you can remember to bring up the subject. But, you may want to print up some business cards or even advertise in the news paper. You might offer a lost and found service this way, depending on your tolerance for odd calls from people whom you do not know. You never know until you try it. As mentioned before, marina owners know about items lost around their slips and refueling units and could recommend you to retrieve lost objects

Offering help to your local police department can aid law enforcement and heighten your reputation. Many detecting clubs offer this service and motivated individuals can too. It is a great way to build a rapport with your local officials and can add to your lead list. These are the best people to have on your side after all.

I made up some eye catching business cards to hand out to those folks that are always stopping me while detecting with questions.

This gives me a chance to better answer their question and sometimes add to my lead list, which develop into hunting opportunities. I also pin these cards on those corkboards in restaurants in new areas I travel to. Be sure to add your cell phone number and email address to field casual questions from curious folks that may be interested in you searching their property. Also place the cards at areas that people will see as lost and found items, like college laundry mats, rec camps and marinas.

Anonymity and Treasure Hunting go hand in hand. Professional treasure hunters seldom, if ever, announce their successful recoveries. Publicity brings with it huge hurdles and attracts the curious sightseer as well as government authorities. Your problems compound with the need of securing legal aid and home security. Regardless of how large (or small) the discovery is, people will blow this story out of proportion. The popular presumption is that you recovered more than you recorded. If this discovery was on private property, (which you have permission to search, of course) the landowner may not enjoy his new popularity with sightseers, thus damaging his property and your relationship with him.

Found money has a way of bring out the worst in some people. Regardless of how much time and resources were used to make the recovery, it is discarded as easy money, and somehow everyone is entitled to a portion. This is especially true of state and federal officials. How can we find out about the laws affecting Treasure hunting? Again research can be helpful if your town Library has a few law books on hand. You may also call someone at the government agency that oversees the particular area you plan to hunt about any restrictions to searching and above all, get permission to hunt private land.

Chapter Twelve: Putting it All Together

By now you have figured out what you are most interested in and have some ideas on where to start, or you may be well on your way to a future in Treasure Hunting. You just need to put it all together and go out and do it. The journey of a thousand miles start with the first step. Many include their family or those trusted friends and search locally their whole career. Others scramble around with too little time at dream destinations and hope for top performance. The choice is all yours.

Few ever get rich at this-and a few do. The values grow with experience and over time accumulate. The greatest value is just being free to pursue your interest. The greatest Treasure- is being an independent thinking American. We are allowed to work hard towards our goals and devote our energy to fulfilling those dreams. We can venture into uncharted regions or languish quietly at home. A veritable smorgasbord of opportunity has been afforded you, the prestige of independence. Plan a vacation around your interest and the interest of your family, and increase the adventure from that performance. Enjoy the simple things in life.

This could be a hedge against inflation as well. Depending on your devotion to the venture, your region, the local history and intrinsic value of your finds, they could help recession proof your household during lean times. Or they can be kept for future consideration and a form of retirement. Our whole retirement plan revolves around Treasure Hunting and traveling to all of those places we wanted to go but didn't have the time.

This works well in the "Autumn" of your life. After you have raised your family and have an empty nest, you have much more time on your hands. Considerable opportunities reveal themselves when you slow down to notice them. A Treasure attitude always notices more. A practical and versatile lifestyle may very well extend your life as well.

A Few Final Thoughts:

All major metal detector manufactures feature and sell the newest machines available, many will also have good used detectors but are reluctant to sell the lower priced items. Inquire about their trade-in programs and the good quality used detectors. Many a good metal detector can be found on eBay, some with very little hours on them. As for detector brands, pick a quality manufacturer who has been in the business a long time, such as Whites, Garrett, Fisher, Bounty Hunter, or Minelab.

Now that detectors have all of the bells and whistles, and tell you what you may have found before you even dig, people are passing over targets as unworthy to dig. Many are passing up the deep targets as troublesome. I found the greatest items back when I had to dig the target up to identify it. These features are to aid in your search, not to determine if you are to dig or not. You will find items of greater value the deeper you go, so do not pass on those deep hard to find objects.

When detectors only offered VHF/TR, we used a method to identify good targets called reverse discrimination. While searching in the motion mode, one would receive a signal and pinpoint it, then turn the mode to TR, push the threshold button to zero, then very slowly move the coil away from the target.

If the threshold sound dropped off to nothing, then this was a target that needed to be dug-up. Very often, this was the difference between failure and success. I have not heard this method mentioned in a long time.

Caches - Finding a cache is perhaps the single greatest discovery for a Treasure hunter, especially the landlocked landlubber. They seem to be found so seldom, you'd think they were rarely hidden. The fact is, cache exist in great numbers. One author I've read suggests 1 in 4 homesteads have a cache of value. Caches were a necessity of daily frontier life. Banks, the government insured and protected type, are a modern luxury. People today haven't known mass banking failures like the last depression, and banks are everywhere. Our target homestead was far removed from any early bank and it was trusted, well, about as far as you could throw one. That only left hiding your money somewhere around close at hand. Money was needed less often, but often enough that it needed to be accessible. More times than not, the hider of the stash never shared the location with anyone, insuring its safety. This also insured the fact that this cache is still on the property....somewhere.

These are also the most challenging treasures to locate, with the exception of hidden Spanish mines. Would you have hidden your stash inside the main house or outside? Would you hide it inside of a building or in the ground? Your guess is as good as mine, but, you need to search both (if possible). The book "Search" by James R. Warnke is a very good book for your search. It covers the house, yard, and property search.

I carefully start inside, at the top, with a strong light and cover everything with the beam from the light. Think, try to tune-in to the property. Investigate all loose boards, blindsides and corners, and any string or wire disappearing from sight (like down an inside wall or door frame).

Small pin pointer detectors or hand scanners work well here, but will find nails and such.

Another tool and skill you should develop is dowsing. This can narrow down your search area and speed up the process greatly. This ancient art once was the only way to locate precious metals, water or anything else the seeker wished to find. Many still call the device a Spanish needle. Many a water-witcher out performs today's well driller. Dowsing is a gift or sixth sense that few realize they possess or can tap into because they lack the faith to even try. Still others are ignorant to the facts. If you have 160 areas to search, why not narrow the search to a smaller area as quick as possible. There are a number of companies and dealers who sell modern dowsing devices powered by crystals, batteries or some other exotic power source to boost the users inherit ability. The secret is to have a treasure attitude. There is treasure out there and you are going to find it. The fact that you are looking has you halfway there.

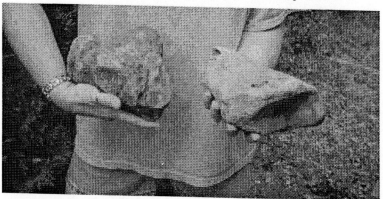

Fossilized bones found in Southeast Texas.

Caches won't always be money either. You may find canning jars, bottles, marbles, hand tools, horse tack, and antique guns. All of these items have great value somewhere; you just need to develop that worth. The possibilities are endless, but you have to be able to recognize it when you see it.

A Different kind of Treasure...

Many of us have found Indian arrowheads and spear points while detecting. It just happens because we are looking where the search coil is going. Sometimes we even find semi-precious stones with no metallic qualities. But, what about prehistoric fossils or dinosaur bones? You don't have to be a Paleontologist to find these ancient treasures. I have a very good friend who searches sand bars in a predominate river waterway for fossilized dinosaur bones. He uses a boat to get him from sandbar to sandbar and simply walks them in his search for bones, bone fragments, teeth, antlers, you name it. It is amazing the huge amount of material he has gathered over the years. He began by accident, and then researched the items he had recovered. Research can work both ways. There is now a growing market for these fossils on eBay.

Many coastal areas have petrified shark teeth washing up on them. Some are from the large prehistoric shark "mega mouth". Teeth as large as a man's hand have been discovered, so keep a treasure eye out for this.

Meteorites. We all have seen the shooting star at night, but few know a meteorite when we come upon one. The rub is, they sell for as much as $1000 per gram and are in high demand, especially among museums and universities. Some folks only hunt for these with their detectors and everything else they find is a nuisance. There are three basic types of meteor; stony, iron, and stony-iron. Some areas make the search for meteorites easier and others add to the difficulty. Check your local library and see how many books are available about these stony space rocks.

Old Photos and Films. These treasures freeze time as it was at that very moment and are desired by many, the hard part is getting the right party with right celluloid. Museums and universities are always a good place to check, but other interested parties may pay more. Films of famous people always get the public excited. Video, films, or old photos of unusual or bizarre phenomena get everybody excited. Phenomena such as the notorious Lock Ness monster, Bigfoot and UFO's must be worth something. Finding these can be a by product of cleaning out attics and garages, or they can be passed down from one generation to the next. It's up to you to find them.

Dumpster Diving. Hearing this, some people think of scavenging though garbage dumpster of nasty restaurant refuse and trash. It's much more than that - but that's fun too. Obviously you can find recyclable metals like aluminum cans and plumber's copper pipes and fittings, or returnable bottles. With flea markets and garage sales, there is a whole new opportunity to find items of interest or value. Many folks will hold a couple of garage sales and throw out unsold items instead of packing them back up. Some times people simply throw-out many books, magazines, papers and such without investigating them thoroughly. Sometimes value items will be tossed by accident. How about industrial dumpsters? Growing up on a whole sale nursery, we recycled many items not suitable to sale. A Can factory had piles of rejected cans that were great for planting starters in. A Door factory had piles of saw dust or wood chips that we used in a dirt mix at the nursery. There are many examples but I'll stop here.

Amateur Treasure Hunters can excel in any of these areas and slowly build on these experiences. Skill and some degree of luck will reward the persistent searcher.

Finding silver and collectable coins in bank bags. Seldom are silver coins found today in change exchanged in normal activities. Sometimes you may find a silver dime near the end of the month- some poor fixed-income elderly person had to spend to meet the grocery bill. Others may have also been fortunate to receive the same thing but didn't recognize their blessing, thus returning it into the system or in to the banks.

Going to large banks and purchasing bank bags of coins is a way to improve your odds of finding some out of circulation coins. Banks sell per-count bags for normal change in everyday business, dimes, quarters and halfs in one hundred dollar bags.

Avoid new sewn closed bags from the mint that will just contain new minted money. These are worth searching for mint quality new coins and also mint errors or mistakes, but not for silver coins. The older, bank filled bags have a better chance of containing silver coinage.

This is not as good as it was years ago when clad money made its introduction. I remember my Dad bringing home bags of quarters and half-dollars to find the silver still in circulation in 1965 and 1966. He found a great amount of silver coins, but they were disappearing fast. "Bad money always forces out good money", is a phrase for good reason - it's true. Much of these coins were liquidated in the 1979-1980 period when silver went to a high of $48 per Oz. Many coins were melted down then or sold for melt. This means that those that remain in collections today will be worth more sooner or later.

Final Word

Treasure hunting is a hobby for most of us, and above all, it should be fun. Some of my least productive days have been the most fun. Having fun at all you do will be its own reward.

I lay no claim to be any great discoverer and will never amount to a Mel Fisher or Robert Marx or Charles Garrett. But I will find more than my fair share, work hard at finding it and enjoy myself doing it. Finding more with less will be my mantra and life long ambition.

As for writing this book, I have so much to say and no way to get it all down in a coherent sentence. I just hope it makes some sense and helps you find treasure that has been long over looked. And I hope your treasures enrich your life and those around you. I hope you fill your own treasure chest to the brim with gold and silver, and what ever other riches you may find. Some of those riches will be the people you meet along the way and the growth of your experience.

May you live long and prosper and always see gold in the bottom of your scoop.

Twenty-five Essential Books for the Well-Read Treasure Hunter

"The New Successful Coin Hunting" by Charles Garrett

"Advanced Water Working Techniques" by Andy Sabisch

"Coin and Relic Dredging" by R. L. Smith

"Hurricane Treasure, 1715 Beach Sites" by Kevin Reilly, Gart Rowe and Kevin Maranville

"The Beach Bank, Your Treasure Tiller" by Kevin Reilly

"Treasure Hunter's Field Notebook" by Mike "Hawkeye" Pickett

"Shipwrecks in the Americas" by Robert Marx

"Treasure under Your Feet" by Roy Volker and Dick Richmond

"They Found Treasure" by Robert F. Burgess

"Pieces of Eight- Recovering the Riches of a Lost Spanish Treasure Fleet" by Kip Wagner and L. B. Tayor Jr.

"Modern Treasure Hunting" by Charles Garrett

"The New Modern Detectors" by Charles Garrett

"Sunken Treasure: How to Find It" by Bob Marx

"Treasure Recovery from Sand and Sea" by Charles Garrett

"The Pirate Prince" by Barry Clifford

"Search" by James R. Warnke

"Treasure Hunter, Undiscovered Treasures of the Southwest" by Jerry Williams

"In Search of the Civil War" by Bob Tervillian

"Electronic Prospecting" by Charles Garrett

"Treasure Hunting Pays Off" by Charles Garrett

"Buried Treasure in the United States" by Robert Marx

"Weekend Prospecting" by Roy Lagal

"Sunken Ships and Treasure" by John Christopher Fine

"Shallow Water Treasure Hunting Manual" by Robert Granville

"Treasure of the Spanish Main" by Lund Humphries

"The Search for the Atocha" by Eugene Lyon

"Quest for Treasure" by Robert Marx

"Diamonds in the Surf" by Bob Trevillian and Frank Carter

"The Poor Man's Treasure Hunter" by Bob Trevillian and Frank Carter

"Lost Treasure of the Florida's Gulf Coast" by L. Frank Hudson and Gordon R. Perscott

"The Beach Hunter's Treasure Guide" by Robert Granville

"Treasure Trove, Where to Find Great Lost Treasure of the World" by Tim Haydock

Notes

Notes

Notes

Printed in the United States
42032LVS00005B/21

9 780741 419057